Becoming a Life Coach

The Comprehensive Guide to Life Coaching

Table of Contents

Becoming a Life Coach 1

Introduction 3

Chapter 1: Brief introduction about life coaching 5

Chapter 2: Skills, abilities and essential knowledge required 12

Chapter 3: Employment outlook and projections as a career 20

Chapter 4: Becoming a certified life coach 28

Chapter 5: Focus of a complete life coach 36

Chapter 6: Extra tips to have in mind 41

Conclusion 45

Introduction

This book contains proven steps and strategies on how to become a truly inspirational master in the art of life coaching. The skills, abilities and knowledge that you already possess should be altered in a certain way to enjoy the fruits of success in life coaching.

If you do not develop your ability to do all this and coach yourself to become a better life coach, you will never be able to reach the point of excellence in the field of life coaching.

It's time for you to become an amazing life coach who can help people to change and adapt to the different possibilities of life with a positive outlook and daring sense. It is time for you to become a master life coach and help people to master their own way of life.

Chapter 1: Brief introduction about life coaching

Life in general is made of constant changes that are unavoidable and hard to miss out on. Change is something that keeps all the people move on towards other good things in life. This adaptation to change is accepted and utilized by most of the people and they welcome a change with a smile and open arms in excitement and a rush to feel something new.

This positive outlook to change is not universal and there are many who have a very tough time in trying to cope up with these types of changes. Those who fear these changes and find it hard to adopt with them tend to miss out on the beautiful possibility of enhancing their own way of life. And these are the people who need help while dealing with these types of changes.

So basically life coaching is a kind of counseling or coaching that can be utilized smartly to guide and help people who are in the crossroads of their lives. Life coaches help them through the major changes that they go through. Life coach professionals guide people to plan their goals and take efforts to reach those goals.

The reasons for seeking help from a professional life coach are many and their essential goal is to move forward and utilize the possibilities of change. The different phases of life in which life coaches' guidance is considered important are:

- ✓ While choosing a college after finishing high school
- ✓ While thinking about beginning a career option

- ✓ While trying to advance in a career field
- ✓ While coping with the after effects of a broken relationship
- ✓ While trying to move into a new home at a new place
- ✓ While trying to reorganize and plan the long term and short term financial goals
- ✓ While trying to achieve personal goals such as gaining weight or getting fit.

There are some traits, skills and abilities to have if you want to become a master in life coaching. You should be full of energy with an ability to motivate, inspire and organize smartly. You should also possess some very good communication skills including the habit of listening patiently.

This practice and field of life coaching has been in existence for the past few years and the field got its popularity between late 70's and early 80's. Forms of various life coaching such as business coaching and executive coaching were used to guide professional executives, managers and CEOs to communicate better and improve career wise. The transition to life coaching in general made its way in the 90's. Life coaching is now useful for everyone and it is available too.

Need of life coaching:

It is essential to guide the lost ones in the right path during and after a major change in life. Those who are unable to accept the transition will find it very hard to move forward in life. This brings in the necessity of life coaching to help and guide anyone to go through the various highs and lows in life. A professional life coach can guide and help these kinds of people to move on in life to have a better life.

Functions of a life coach:

- Life coaches guide all kinds of people in all phases of lives. Some of them focus only on a certain group of people or on a certain situation.

- A good life coach is a good sounding board to the clients. A life coach is always expected to listen patiently to the troubles of the clients.

- A good life coach perceives with an unbiased eye and a brave perspective. This makes the life coach to help the client go through various hurdles in life.

- A life coach holds an in depth interview before dealing with the client. He/she extracts the clients' needs, wants and goals that they want to achieve in the future.

- A life coach knows that every person is different and life coaching is an individualized process. The steps and techniques that a life coach uses on a client might not work on another.

- He/she brings up plans according to the strength, weakness, limits and abilities of the client along with their values and morals.

- A good life coach keeps track of the progress of the clients. He/she allots them action-oriented works that are made to guide them in the right direction towards the goal.

- He/she thrives for accountability from the clients and also becomes a source of motivation and inspiration.

Life coaches find employment opportunities with universities and large corporations. There are many firms that employ life coaches for the sole purpose. But most of them work independently by following their own way of practice. There are also teams of life coaches that provide a broad range of services with good quality.

There are no vital educational requirements as such to take this up a career. You might not even need a certificate or a license to do this. But some life coaches think that a proper education is vital for a professionally well setup career. There are various paths to choose from when you take life coaching as a profession. You can also find lots of certificate programs to help you become a life coach.

It is very hard to guess a salary of a life coach. Life coaches earn between 25, 000 dollars to 200,000 dollars. This broad range in earnings is due to factors such as the ability of an individual to attract clients and the rate of competition within the same field.

Chapter 2: Skills, abilities and essential knowledge required

Unlike other social work fields such as psychology and counseling, this doesn't necessarily need a degree or a period of training to practice professionally. You need not tread deeply into topics such as behavioral problems, anthropology, counseling, statistic, sociology or psychology.

But you have to place yourself as a specialist if you have to achieve success in it. A financial life coach would be in high demand if he/she is an expert in the area of finances, markets, taxes and trades. There a lot of areas to specialize in ranging from simple career coaching to the risky affair of dealing with substance abuse and relationships.

Another trouble while taking this as a profession is that it is not regulated and anyone can claim to be a life coach. This affects the quality of life coaching all around the world. The constant fluctuation of quality from one life coach to another will easily make the clients to lose trust and interest in it. So an accreditation as a certified life coach can attract more clients and strengthen the relation with old clients for your own good.

You should know and be knowledgeable about a versatile range of topics. You should be able to talk with anyone about anything. Being a life coach, you can get into the payroll of large and successful multinational companies. You can also opt to work in an office environment or prefer to travel around while doing your work. They might or might not have an experience in all the fields. They are experts who guide individual or groups to develop personally or in different areas of profession.

Essential knowledge of the following things I vital for this profession and they are:

- **General knowledge:** Knowledge about a certain specific topic or knowledge about many topics. This is really vital if you consider career coaching as your specialization.

- **Psychological principle knowledge:** This knowledge is not really necessary, but a basic psychological knowledge would prove to be helpful in figuring out the various differences in the way in which people behave, get motivated and feel inspired.

- **Communication:** You have to talk and communicate with various types of people from different walks of lives. It is essential that you have a good communication skill with clarity and a good knowledge in the language.

Fluency in various languages is a great add-on.

- **Knowledge of teaching:** You should be able to teach clearly by using variety of techniques. You have to extract, enhance and showcase different ideas and solutions in the right way to make people understand.

- **Positivity and self assurance:** You should possess a certain flair and confidence in your ability to guide your clients in the perfect way. You should have a very good positive attitude and it should be reflected in your attitude, approach, tone, way of speaking and way of writing.

- **Urge to know more and research oriented skills:** There are lots of changes that happen every day with new laws, rapid growth of research and market transformation. You should follow all these changes in the field of life coaching and you should look into new possibilities and opportunities that arrive out of it.

- **Practical knowledge:** You should possess the knack of assessing and transforming thoughts into actions for the purpose of client's improvement. You should be practical, smart and positive about life.

Along with an urge to help and guide people, a good life coach should possess a very good listening and communication skill. He/she should also have a very good knowledge in the areas that he/she chooses to cover as a life coach. If you have a work experience in the social service sector, you can guide and coach clients in dealing with stress, relationships and substance abuse.

Other skills and abilities that can prove to be worthy and good to a life coach are:

- **Skills to organize:** When you become a life coach, you have to see and talk with numerous clients on a single working day. Your busy schedule will need perfect organization if you want to attract more clients.

- **Skills to motivate:** You should be able to inspire and motivate your clients to embrace the change and make something out of it. You should be able to extract the essence of a person's potential if you want to become a successful life coach.

- **Ability to be flexible:** A good life coach should be flexible and easy to approach. You should allow your clients to go through their own personal transitions individually and not with a group. You should be able to work with each one of them personally to bring out a better result.

- **Showing empathy:** A good life coach should not judge and should not make assumptions based on what he/she sees. You should not be judgmental and instructional. You should be empathetic towards your clients and listen to them with patience.

- **Self-assuring trait:** A life coach motivates and pushes other people to transform for their own good in personal and professional phases of life. You should be very confident in your ability to coach them and guide them properly. Confidence in your ability to guide them in the right path is very important to be a successful life coach.

- **Positive approach:** A good life coach should always be charming and positive while approaching the client. Life coaches should have an alluring tone and attitude that makes the people to trust and believe in.

- **Touch of creativity:** Creativity is absolutely essential in all kinds of profession. You should be able to come up with exciting new ideas for your clients. You should have a touch of insane creativity to make sure that you get the results you craved for.

Chapter 3: Employment outlook and projections as a career

Many people assume that the professional side of life coaching is a new field that has come up in recent times, but the truth is that life coaching has been a profession in formal ways since the 1950's and it was then called as business coaching. During those times, it focused only on guiding corporate managers and CEOs to enhance their professional performance for better efficiency in the output.

But right now there are numerous career opportunities to be a life coach. The International Coach Federation identifies various coaching specialties that include spirituality, relationships, fitness, business and weight management. According to a job forum website, a professional life coach earns an average fee of 36 dollars each hour and the Forbes article once stated that life coaches have the ability to gross 100,000 dollars on an annual basis.

- ➢ The pay in this profession is based on two very important factors- and they are experience on the field and time put on the job. If you want to earn more, you have put in extra effort and time on the job.

- ➢ The location of the life coach also plays another vital role. You can't possibly be a life coach in the middle of the desert or at the quaint old country side. Placement of your office or workspace is important when you want to become a successful life coach.

- ➢ Life coaches mostly don't have benefits like medical insurance or retirement funds unless they are financed in the personal level.

- Females make up most of the life coaching professionals around the globe.

- The satisfaction of doing the work is good and most life coaches really love what they do. This makes it a very interesting job with a bonus of meeting different types of people from all walks of life.

- It is fun and not mundane because you would have the flexibility to work anytime and anywhere. Time is not at all an issue and if you can't meet your client personally you can also complete your session over phone or other voice-to-voice communication platforms.

- You would have the opportunity to work with various kinds of clients. The range in variety is broad and it is one of the positives of being a life coach. You will never get bored.

Today it has become very common and you can see life coaches dealing in various types of fields and from different backgrounds. Life coaches come from different sources and they are from various professional fields like teaching, human resources, army/police, healthcare, therapy and counseling.

According to the survey made by the federation, over 40% of the professional certified and trained life coaches believe that untrained coaches without proper certification are the greatest factor of worry in the growing industry. They are afraid that the untrained ones would bring down the quality of service provided in the society.

Certification to be a life coach:

There are numerous agencies that help in turning you into a certified life coach such as

IAC (International Association for Coaching) and ICF (International Coach Federation). There are two of the well known organizations that help in turning you into a certified and professional life coach.

To get this certification, you must be able to crack an oral test and a written examination. The process also includes submission of coaching sessions that are recorded to showcase your own knowledge and the ability to apply it practically. The certification from ICF is hard to finish and it takes time because you must have practiced coaching for a certain number of paid hours before getting the certification.

There is no need of a separate degree program to become a life coach and practice it. Getting proper amount of training in different fields can help you in the profession and it can enhance the chances for a good pay from clients.

You should attend various weekend workshops, classes and training schools to get better in various skills such as client-coach relationships, goal setting skills and communication skills. These skills are essential in helping you get better in this field.

Before you get into this field professionally and seriously, you should consider taking part in coach-training programs to identify your level of skills in life coaching. You should also connect with other experienced life coaches and ask for their guidance and advice to improve in your areas of interest.

Employment opportunities for life coaches:

A life coach should understand the general principles that can lead to success. He/she must know how to practically apply the principles and guide others in an efficient way.

There are numerous areas to pursue when you are a life coach and they are:

- Field of career coaching where you can provide guidance for working professionals and help them during transition. Career coaches are hired in many multinational companies to help out their employees deal with changes in lives and profession.

- Business and corporate coaching where you can focus on managers and guide them for better management. Upper management coaching is a lot more professional and high-end.

- Executive coaching where you can focus on business executives to improve their business.

- Spiritual coaching where you can guide and help people with the tools of spirituality.

- Weight and body image coaching in which you can help people to get fit and look good with a good health and beauty balance. Lot of people wants to get fit these days and they seek the help of life coaches for the same.

- Work-life balance coaching is a field in which you can guide your clients to have a good work-life balance.

- Relationship coaching where you deal with clients going through relationship problems in life.

- Time management coaching makes you to deal with people who would want to improve their time management skills.

Chapter 4: Becoming a certified life coach

To become a certified life coach, you should do the following things:

- Get ready to be a coach
- Avail the best training for becoming a life coach
- Keep on practicing your life coaching skills
- List yourself with different directories for the clients to find you
- Embrace the whole thing

Getting ready to be a coach:

You can become a model coach by joining with an accredited mentor coach. Before you get committed into that, you should coach yourself by reading and knowing a lot about it. Check online for courses that help in coaching yourself and get your own life in the right path at first. Read more books on the same topic and increase your knowledge on the subject. You should be ready to be a coach and you should be courageous enough to take the leap without worrying about failures.

Availing the best training for becoming a life coach:

If you enjoyed working with another accredited life coach, you should take the next step and get some training at an ICF recognized training program. Visit their website to know a lot about these programs.

Practicing your life coaching skills:

Once you enroll yourself in a proper training platform, make sure that you practice your skills with clients. Start by coaching your acquaintances that are willing to volunteer. Once you reach a good number of hours under practice you will get the confidence and a level of professionalism to coach other people.

Listing yourself with different directories for the clients to find you:

After enrolling in an ICF recognized training program, you will be able to list in various directories as a professional "coach under training". This will definitely help you in getting new clients for exposure. You can also offer to coach for free or for a discount rate to get some practice and exposure. If you have full time day job, do not think about quitting it. It might take a year or two to complete the coach training program.

Embracing the whole thing:

It takes years to complete the training and become a certified life coach. You shouldn't rush it and make it as mess. Keep improving your skills by practicing and exposure. Enjoy the whole thing and take it steady and slow.

Some of the life coaching programs and courses are:

- The Clean Sweep Program
- Online courses like "Coach yourself to success"
- An audio program called "The secret laws of attraction"
- 1:1 private mentor coaching program

Becoming a certified life coach:

Certified coaches guide their clients to obtain their personal or professional goals through a mixture of process that includes process of self-assessment, goal setting and getting solutions. To get a life coaching certificate a combination of good formal training and exposure is essential.

1. Process of self-assessment
2. Finishing an accredited training program for life coaching
3. Completing the necessary coaching hours
4. Seeking other educational options

Process of self-assessment:

To be an efficient life coach, you should have some core competencies with you. You should go through an initial self-assessment test to make sure that life coaching is a suitable career option for you. According to the ICF, the core competencies are:

- Good listening skills
- Very strong communication skills
- Genuine concern and care towards others' improvement
- Good creativity
- Smart problem solving ability
- Good progress management

These core competencies are a must-have and if you think you do not possess any of these traits, you should think about improving yourself before you get down to start helping others.

Finishing an accredited training program for life coaching:

Certification from the ICF is widely recognized among all the other certifications available. It offers various levels of certification that includes the PCC (Professional Certified Coach), MCC (Master Certified Coach) and ACC (Associate Certified Coach).

These certifications need a mixture of proper training, coaching exposure, examinations and references from accredited coaches. The subjects that are taught here include communication, relationships with the clients, finding out limiting beliefs, organizational behavior, professional ethics and decision making.

Completing the necessary coaching hours:

The exposure and the experience is a vital element for certification. ICF requires you to complete and record 100 to 2,500 hours of coaching depending on various levels of certification. And most of the coaching hours should be paid.

This requirement for experience can be obtained by individual coaching, coaching through a 3rd party organization, internal coaching and group coaching. Coaching can be done personally face-to-face or by telephonic conversations or by any other voice-to-voice communication medium.

Seeking other educational options:

A continuous flow of education is necessary if you want to achieve well in the field and develop. It is also a necessity if you want to renew your certification. The International Coach Federation requires you to complete 40 hours of continuing education in the period of every three years to renew the certification.

You can opt to attend graduate schools. You need not have to complete an advanced degree program to do this. You can get additional education and knowledge through various graduate level courses that can help you to develop your skills.

Chapter 5: Focus of a complete life coach

A focus of a life coach should be built on the ability to connect with people and the passion to help them out. A life coach should make a powerful difference in the client's life and bring about a change for the betterment of the client.

There are several programs that give you the necessary education and skills to become a very successful life coach. By combining personal training and practical knowledge, you can achieve a lot in this field without breaking a sweat.

Life coaching can focus on various types of people like:

- ✓ **Independent individuals:** This is where a life coach completely focuses on an independent individual to guide that person in the right way for personal gain or professional gain.

- ✓ **Groups:** A life coach can also work on a group of people and guide them in the right direction to produce efficient work results or reach team goals together.

- ✓ **Couples:** Life coaching also focuses on couples with same goals to work on relationships and other changes that come from relationships.

When you become a certified life coach, you will have to help and guide the clients who reach you for a sense of direction when all the paths seem to be hopeless and bad. As a coach, your help should induce these changes in the clients and they are:

- **Clarity and focus:** You should be completely clear and focused about the life that your client has. Without proper clarity and focus on their lives, you will not have the clarity to guide them in the right way.

- **Defined goals and plan of actions:** You should have a defined goal and you should build a plan to achieve those goals. The plan should be clear and practical too. You should explain the plan to your clients and they should believe in it to work out.

- **Achieving the potential:** You must find their complete potential and you must look for ways to make them utilize their potential with all their energy and positivity.

- **Triggering their creativity:** You should find the possibilities of a flow of creativity in them and trigger it to make it work out for them. You should work on to expand their creativity in all the other phases of their lives.

- **Solutions to challenges:** You should make them identify solutions to their problems in life by themselves. They should be courageous and daring enough to face them all with might.

- **No problems only opportunities:** They should be in a clear and focused state of mind that they only see opportunities out of every situation in life instead of focusing on problems.

- **Happy lives:** Your clients should be able to lead a very happy and successful life by overcoming all the hurdles and troubles in life.

By tapping into this field, you can also build a good future financially and make a great difference in other people's lives. As a certified life coach, you have the power to:

- Create and develop a business on your own terms with your own ideals.

- You can have your own schedule and enjoy a stress-free life.

- You can make a career out of it and build a lifestyle that you really love.

- You can touch other people's lives and bring a difference.

Chapter 6: Extra tips to have in mind

- Life coaching in companies is more than just a perk. When it is done in the right way, it can improve the sales, engagement, creativity, satisfaction and results in a workplace.

- A good coach should always bring in a positive change in the clients' lives. You should recognize the individual goals of the clients and work on them to achieve them.

- An efficient coach should work together with the clients and guide them to lead a better and richer life. The change in their lives should not make them scared or anxious. Your clients should be excited and curious about what is coming next. You should make them to reach that level with your guidance.

- It is not only for people with problems. It can also help in sharpening the skills of an individual and identify the skills that they don't know that they have.

- A good life coach should focus on the strength of the individual and look to help him achieve more with what he has.

- A good coach doesn't fix anyone, but he/she helps them to take a path towards a good future.

- It doesn't take too much of your time. Each session lasts 20 to 60 minutes. You need not spend the whole day on a single client. But you can meet 4 to 5 different clients on a single day and carry out a session with each of them to make sure that you aren't bored.

- You are not a friend to your clients. You should want the best from your clients and you should work with them to help them attain their goals. You should challenge your clients and encourage them to do more.

- Life coaching is not only meant for a certain group of people. It is good for anyone who is driven to make a better life and a better future. It brings out the potential in people and encourages them to perform larger.

- The difference between a bad coach and a good coach is that a bad coach is always giving out advices and suggestions. A good coach should allow the client to get out of his/her comfort zone and explore the possibilities. A good coach should come up with ideal choices for the client to choose from. You should be an expert at the subject of changing behavior and the way it affects life.

- Professional coaching is not at all spiritual. It should be practical and meaningful to change people's lives for their own good and betterment.

Conclusion

I hope this book was able to help you to become a master life coach with an ability to change people's lives.

The next step is to put these plans into actions and transform yourself into a master life coach.